WOMEN OF
THE MIDDLE EAST

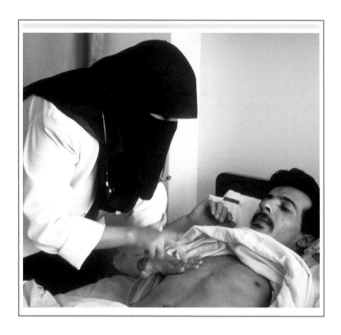

By Sheila Rivera

VISIT US AT
WWW.ABDOPUB.COM

Published by ABDO & Daughters, an imprint of ABDO Publishing Company, 4940 Viking Drive, Suite 622, Edina, Minnesota 55435. Copyright ©2004 by Abdo Consulting Group, Inc. International copyrights reserved in all countries. No part of this book may be reproduced in any form without written permission from the publisher.

Printed in the United States.

Edited by: Cory Gunderson
Contributing Editors: Chad Morse, Chris Schafer
Graphic Design: Arturo Leyva, David Bullen
Cover Design: Castaneda Dunham, Inc.
Photos: Corbis

Library of Congress Cataloging-in-Publication Data

Rivera, Sheila, 1970-
    Women of the Middle East / Sheila Rivera.
      p. cm. -- (World in conflict--The Middle East)
    Includes index.
    Summary: Explores the roles and responsibilities of women throughout the Middle East, including how religion, marriage, and politics influence their lives.
    Contents: Overview of women of the Middle East -- Women in Afghanistan -- Women in Egypt -- Women in Iran -- Women in Israel -- Women in Saudi Arabia.
      ISBN 1-59197-415-1
      1. Women--Middle East--Juvenile literature. 2. Women--Middle East--Social conditions--Juvenile literature. [1. Women--Middle East. 2. Women--Middle East--Social conditions.] I. Title. II. World in conflict. Middle East.

    HQ1726.5.R58 2003
    305.42'0956--dc21
                                                                    2003044377

TABLE OF CONTENTS

Afghan women wearing burqas

OVERVIEW OF WOMEN IN THE MIDDLE EAST

Women in the Middle East have specific roles within their societies. They have certain responsibilities within the family. They fit differently into the workforce than men. They have different roles in their countries' governments.

Women's roles in Middle Eastern societies are similar, but there are distinct differences in women's rights from one country to the next.

Religion influences many of the laws that govern women in the Middle East. Some countries are governed by religious laws. Others have governments that are not religion-based, but they leave certain issues to be determined by religious laws. Some families punish their own family members for breaking religious laws.

Most Middle Eastern societies hold women responsible for cooking, caring for the children, and doing household chores. Many of them expect men to support the family financially.

Marriage is valued in all Middle Eastern countries. Some countries do not allow women to interact with men outside of the family, so parents arrange marriages for their children. In some Middle Eastern countries, girls can give their opinions of prospective husbands. Not all countries in the region give girls a choice.

Middle Eastern opinions on women in the workforce vary. In one Middle Eastern country, some women have to work so their husbands can study religious texts. In others, the idea of women working outside the home is looked down upon.

While many Middle Eastern countries claim that women have equal rights to men, there are obvious differences in their treatment. In many Middle Eastern countries, women cannot leave the house if they are not wearing the proper clothes. Some are not allowed to drive cars. Others are not allowed to work in certain jobs or in government.

In some Middle Eastern countries, women have many of the rights men do. Some can vote and have equal rights to education.

A Middle Eastern woman cares for her child.

Some Middle Eastern women are allowed to participate in the military. Some are also able to hold government positions. A woman has even been elected to lead one Middle Eastern nation.

While many restrictions are placed on some Middle Eastern women, not everyone views these restrictions negatively. Some women who live in the Middle East trust in their religion so much that they willingly accept the restrictions placed on them. Some think that too much freedom is bad.

The following chapters describe the roles of women in five Middle Eastern countries. The Middle East is made up of many more countries. Those included in this book represent a sampling of the broad range of rights and restrictions that affect women in the region.

AFGHANISTAN

A fghanistan is a country that was once ruled by an Islamic fundamentalist government. Islam is a religion that is based on the holy book, the Koran.

In Afghanistan, women's rights have changed over the years. The way that women have been treated in the last decade has been strongly influenced by the Taliban. The Taliban forced an Islamic fundamentalist government on the Afghan people. Islamic fundamentalism is an extreme form of Islam. Its followers live by a strict interpretation of the Koran. People who do not follow the teachings, as fundamentalists expect, are often brutally punished.

The Taliban ran Afghanistan from 1996 to 2001. In the height of its power, the Taliban controlled 65 to 85 percent of Afghanistan. In 2001, the United States forced the Taliban from power through military force. Even though the Taliban does not rule Afghanistan anymore, its influences are still felt among Afghan people today.

In Afghanistan, the Taliban forced women to wear burqas in public.

During the 1970s and 1980s, before the Taliban controlled Afghanistan, women wore clothes much like women in Western nations. Women worked in agriculture, medicine, and law. Nearly 50 percent of Afghanistan's doctors were women. Seventy percent of teachers in the city of Kabul were women. When the Taliban took power, women were no longer free to dress as they wanted, or to work outside of the home.

Islam states that both women and men have responsibilities to their families. According to Islam, women are responsible for raising the children, and men are responsible for financially supporting the family.

Under Taliban rule, these ideas were taken to the extreme. Women stayed at home to raise the children. The Taliban did not allow them to leave their homes. Women could only leave the house for reasons approved by the government.

The Taliban enforced a strict dress code on women. If a woman left her house, she was required to wear a burqa. A burqa is a piece of clothing that completely covers a woman from head to toe. It looks like a cape with a mesh screen in the front. The screen allows a woman to see out from under her covering. A burqa is heavy and hot to wear. There have been cases in which women in burqas have been hit by cars. They could not see the cars due to limited vision under the burqa.

Burqas are also expensive. The Taliban would not allow women to work, so many women could not afford to buy a burqa. Sometimes women in a neighborhood would share one burqa. They would take turns wearing it. That meant that women could be restricted to their houses for days until it was their turn to wear the burqa.

Since the Taliban left power, women are no longer required to wear burqas. Many women continue to wear them anyway. Some women feel uncomfortable in public without them. They see people looking at their faces, and they feel uneasy. In some areas, like the capital city of Kabul, women continue to wear the burqa out of fear. Some Taliban members still exist in Afghanistan. Women are afraid that they could still be beaten by those people if they are seen without a burqa. Women who don't wear burqas wear veils on their heads, but their faces are exposed. Muslim women wear veils because their religion requires them to.

The Taliban also forbid women to leave their homes unless they were in the company of a male relative. If a woman was seen on the streets alone she was beaten.

In one case, a woman named Torpeka left her home without a male escort because her baby was sick. A Taliban officer told her to stop. She did not stop. She was afraid her child would die. The officer shot her in the back with a machine gun. She survived the attack, and she and her child got medical attention. When a

Afghan women are not allowed in public without a male relative to escort them.

complaint was filed with Taliban authorities, nothing was done. They claimed Torpeka had no right to be outside of her home in the first place.

In another incident, a woman named Sohaila was caught walking with a man who was not a relative. The Taliban beat her in front of 30,000 men and boys in the Olympic Sports Stadium in Kabul. They wanted everyone to see what happened to people who broke their laws.

The Taliban ordered people to pray in the mosque five times a day. This was very difficult for women because of the strict conditions under which they were allowed to leave the house.

In Afghanistan, marriages are arranged. The arrangement is usually made between the parents of the prospective bride and groom. Under Taliban rule, women were sometimes forced into marriages. Fathers in Afghanistan have had their lives threatened if they did not turn their daughters over for marriage. Even though the Taliban is no longer in power, women are still forced into marriage. Parents continue to sell their daughters to future husbands.

Most Afghanis are Sunni Muslims. A Sunni woman is seldom allowed to divorce a man. In Afghanistan, there is one exception to this rule. Courts can allow a woman to divorce her husband if she can prove that she was forced into marriage against her will. It is rare that a woman can prove this, so few are granted a divorce.

Afghan women are expected to care for their children and do housework.

One Afghan woman said, "My father sold me to my husband for a lot of money. I want a divorce and I appeal to the human rights commission to help me." At one point, nearly 800 women were applying to have their marriages terminated every day. Many of them claimed that the Taliban forced them into marriage.

Islam stresses the importance of education for both men and women. Before Taliban rule, women made up half of the students in the university at Kabul. The Taliban forbid women and girls from going to school. Some women took a risk. They taught and studied in secret schools. Now women and girls are free to study again. Almost 80 percent of girls' schools in rural areas were operating as of 2001.

Since the fall of the Taliban, women have begun working again as well. Some have gone back to teaching. There are few job opportunities for women.

The outlook for Afghan women is uncertain. Even though they have regained a few rights, they are still restricted in many ways. Taliban-era ideals still exist. Women still face harassment and threats for not wearing burqas. Women are still sold to their husbands. No one knows for sure what rules the new government will enforce.

Afghan women are allowed in schools once again.

EGYPT

Egypt is a country in the Middle East whose government is separate from religion. Laws are enforced by the government, but religious leaders handle punishment for some offenses.

Many Egyptians have strong ties to their religion. A small percentage practice Christianity or Druze, but most Egyptians are Muslims. They tend to follow the gender-based laws of Islam.

Most Egyptian women raise their families and do the household chores. Some women work outside of the home in addition to these duties. Men are responsible for supporting the family financially.

Egyptian women are in charge of doing all of the cooking for the family. Girls start to help their mothers with the cooking when they are only six or seven years old. Most girls can cook major dishes by the time they are 15 years old. Egyptian women fear that if they cannot cook, their husbands will divorce them. Learning how to cook is a priority.

In Egyptian cities, it is becoming more common for men to share in household duties. In some cases, a family will hire someone to do household chores.

Most Egyptian girls live with their parents until they get married. When a girl gets married, she moves from her parents' house to her husband's house. It is common for Egyptians to arrange marriages, but more and more young women are choosing their own husbands.

In Egypt, it is considered a blessing for a couple to have many children. This is especially true in rural areas where children help adults in the fields. It is also legal for a man to have up to four wives. This is acceptable if he is able to care for them financially and treat them well. Having more than one wife increases the number of children a man can have to help him in the fields. That is why polygamy, or the practice of having more than one wife, is more common in the countryside and within poor communities.

In 2000, a law was passed allowing Egyptian women the right to divorce their husbands. Before that, only men were able to file for divorce. Even in cases of abuse or abandonment, women had to stay married to their husbands until the husband agreed to divorce them. The new law also gives women who divorce the right to child support from the children's father.

Egyptian women are influenced by Western fashion.

According to Islam, if a person shows his or her body, it is seen as tempting to the opposite sex. In order to remain sexually pure, many Egyptian women wear clothes that cover every part of their bodies except their hands and faces.

Muslim women wear long, loose clothing so that men may not define the shape of their bodies and be tempted by them. Many Egyptian women wear veils, or hijab, covering their heads. Women who are highly educated, and those who hold high position jobs, are less likely to wear the hijab than less educated women and women in rural areas. Millions of Egyptian women wear Western dress.

Some people from Western nations think traditional Muslim dress, and the hijab in particular, is restrictive. Some Muslim women wear it with pride. They see the hijab as a symbol of a woman's purity and her respect for God. They wear it to gain respect from other women. They also feel protected from the eyes of men when they are wearing the veil.

A Muslim family's honor depends on the conduct of its female family members. If a woman behaves in a respectful manner, it reflects well on the family. If a woman conducts herself in a way that is not considered respectful, she can bring great shame to her family. This belief has led to the deaths of many women in Egypt and other Middle Eastern countries.

If a Muslim woman is caught, or even suspected of, having sexual relations outside of marriage, she might be killed by her family. This kind of killing is called an honor killing. Some Christians in Egypt also carry out honor killings. People who agree with honor killings think it is better to kill a daughter or wife than to know that others are talking about the shame she has brought to the family.

Honor killing is not legal. Islam does not support it. Islam has rules regarding such conduct. It is up to the religious leaders, not a woman's family, to judge her actions and punish her. Honor killings are not common to all Muslim-dominated countries. They are less common in countries with Islamic governments.

The government has allowed women to participate in the Egyptian workforce since the 1920s. In the 1920s, the Egyptian Feminist Union was created. Its goal was to end the discrimination of women in the workforce. Its power and influence increased in the 1950s. While women can legally work outside of the home, many men look down on it. Even if a woman works outside the home, she is still required to take care of her family and home.

Egyptian women have been able to run for government offices since 1956. That year women gained the right to nominate themselves to the National Assembly for the first time. Since then, the government has even recommended that a certain percentage of government posts be filled by women.

Egypt's most famous feminist, Dr. Nawal al-Saadaw

During his presidency, Anwar Sadat passed legislation regarding women's rights in the Egyptian workforce. He passed a law that required 10 percent of the National Assembly seats to be held by women. In 1984, Egyptian courts abolished that law. Since then, the number of women in the Assembly has dropped from 36 to 5. Many men in Egypt do not approve of women playing major roles in government.

Egypt's constitution gives women equal rights in education, employment, equal pay for equal work, and social security. Egyptian women have been able to vote since 1956.

Just because the law grants women rights, doesn't mean that they can take advantage of these rights. Jobs are often divided by gender. Women hold fewer decision-making positions and high-ranking positions in government than men. Even in other kinds of work, women are less likely to be in decision-making positions. In agriculture, for example, men make almost all of the decisions.

While women in Egypt tend to follow strict religious rules and social codes of conduct, they enjoy some freedoms that other Middle Eastern women do not. The difference in city life versus rural life impacts the degree to which women are constrained. Women's rights in Egypt continue to evolve with time.

IRAN

Like Afghanistan, Iran once had a somewhat liberal government. It was run by Muhammad Reza Shah Pahlavi. Reza was the Shah of Iran for most of the period between 1941 and 1979. He tried to make his country more Westernized. He tried to lessen the role of religion in the Iranian government. He also tried to improve women's rights.

In 1963, Reza gave Iranian women the right to vote for the first time. He encouraged them to work outside the home. He offered women education equal to that offered to men. During Reza's rule, the number of women studying in schools increased from around 185,000 to over two million. Women were able to obtain better jobs in a wider variety of fields.

Reza thought that wearing a veil was restrictive to women, so he abolished the practice.

Many people in Iran did not like Reza's decisions. They felt that he was trying to make the nation too much like Western nations. Some Muslims felt that a Western-like society distracted people from their religion. In 1979, the Iranian people revolted and Reza fled. He was replaced by the Muslim religious leader, the Ayatollah Khomeini.

The Ayatollah Khomeini imposed strict laws on women.

When the Ayatollah Khomeini came to power, he made many changes in Iran. He ruled Iran using the ideas of Islamic fundamentalism. This kind of government, ruled by a religious authority, is called a theocracy. Iran was renamed the Islamic Republic of Iran.

Theocratic fundamentalism views women as physically, intellectually, and morally inferior to men. Under Khomeini's rule, women had fewer rights, and many restrictions were placed on them.

Khomeini's government created laws that gave men the right to make all family decisions. A woman needed her husband's permission before she could go anywhere. According to the religious leader, a woman was considered her husband's slave. Her role in the family was to have and care for children, and to care for her husband.

Under Khomeini's rule, men were allowed to have up to four wives. The legal age for girls to get married changed from 18 years old to nine years old.

Khomeini reintroduced the veil to Iranian society. Under his government, women were required to wear veils that entirely covered their hair and bodies. Only a woman's face and hands were permitted to show. The strict dress code, or hijab, also prohibited women from wearing makeup. Any woman who broke the dress code might be whipped or sent to jail.

Iran

Since Khomeini's death in 1989, Iran has had several presidents. Many of the laws that were set up during Khomeini's rule still affect women today. Iran's current president, Mohammed Khatemi, claimed to have positive views on women before his election in 1997. Many of his policies are restrictive to women.

A married woman cannot travel without written permission from her husband. A single woman must receive written permission from her father.

Iranian law has always allowed a man to divorce his wife. A woman, however, did not have the right to divorce her husband in the past. Although it is still very difficult for a woman to get a divorce, certain conditions will now allow it. A woman may file for a divorce if her husband is violent, has an addiction, or is mentally ill.

In the event of a divorce, custody of the children depends on the age of each child. The children's father receives full custody of any boys over the age of two, and any girls over the age of seven. If the mother marries a different man after the divorce, she loses all custody rights to the children from her previous marriage.

Many of Iran's laws are tied directly to Muslim law, also called Shari'a law. Islam restricts women's activities in order to protect their reputations. The dress code and laws that keep men and women separate are put in place to keep women from tempting men. The harsh punishments further enforce the codes of conduct.

Iran's President, Mohammed Khatemi

Under Shari'a law, adultery, or having sexual relations outside of marriage, is considered a crime. In Iran, a person who is convicted of committing adultery may be killed by stoning. Accused men are buried up to their waists in the earth. Accused women are buried up to their necks. People throw stones at them until they die.

Women in Iran are not free to choose what they wish to study. Many girls drop out of school early because of the young age at which they are married. Once they are married, their responsibility is to care for their husband and family. In some rural areas, the dropout rate for schoolgirls is as high as 90 percent.

In 2001, women gained one significant educational right. Iran's parliament passed a law that allows unmarried women to apply for scholarships to study abroad. Women had not been allowed to do so since 1985.

Women in Iran have few job opportunities. In 2000, only about nine percent of women worked outside of the home. Of that small percentage, 72 percent worked in education. President Khatemi feels that a woman's place is in the home. He has said, "Housekeeping is among one of the most important jobs. The real value of a woman is measured by how much she makes the family environment for her husband and children like a paradise."

In Iran, women are not allowed to interact with men who are not family members. This makes it difficult for a woman to work outside the home even if she wants to. In rural areas, women typically work in agriculture. Others work as teachers, nurses, or secretaries. The women who do manage to work outside the home are paid less than men. Few women become managers or hold high positions in businesses.

Iranian women have been granted government positions, but they are few. In 1997, 13 women were elected to parliament. The highest government position that a woman has held in Iran was President's Advisor on Women's Affairs. President Khatemi also appointed a woman Vice President for Environmental Protection.

In addition to education and job barriers, women in Iran have also faced social restrictions. Until January 2003, women were not allowed to attend any sporting events. The government forbid women from going to games because of the disrespectful language that fans often used. Only in 2003 did a soccer club finally allow women to view a live soccer game. About six women attended the first game since the policy change.

Several women's rights groups have sprung up in Iran. They try to improve women's rights and employment opportunities. Because of their efforts, more women are working in government than in the past.

Iranian women have gone through waves of rights and restrictions. Many of the laws that govern them are influenced by religious laws, which are set up to protect women.

A Jewish wedding ceremony

ISRAEL

srael's government is not a religious government, however, religion strongly influences Israelis' lives. More than 80 percent of Israelis are Jewish. The remaining 20 percent are mostly Christian, Muslim, or Druze. In Israel, many personal matters are left up to religious legislation rather than governmental laws. People can choose to exercise their political rights or to follow the customs of their religion.

Starting a family is important to Jewish people. In Israel, there is a lot of pressure on girls to marry young and start families. Many women give up professional goals. Instead, they choose to get married and have a family. In Jewish families, women care for the children and home. Men must earn a living to support the family.

Some Israelis practice a strict form of Orthodox Judaism. It is called haredi. Within the framework of this group, women are seen as inferior to men. Women often raise the children with

WORLD IN CONFLICT: THE MIDDLE EAST

no help from their husbands. Some haredi men see women's roles so tied to the home that when talking about their wives, a man might call her his "home." Some men in the haredi community do help their wives with the home and children. It can be embarrassing for them if other men see them helping around the house.

In a haredi family, men make most of the decisions. A woman's husband might even decide whether or not his wife will have a social engagement. In some haredi families, men choose to study religious texts rather than work. In such cases, the woman must work to support the family financially. She does this in addition to caring for the family and home.

In Israel, the literacy rate for both men and women is higher than 93 percent. Women have access to higher education. In Israel, women earn more than half of all academic degrees.

Israeli women can vote after they reach 18 years old. Women have been involved in Israel's government for decades. Their participation has been marginal. Since 1948, only six women have held positions in the Israeli cabinet. In the legislature, or Knesset, most of the top positions belong to men. Women usually serve on committees with domestic or social focuses. In 2001, only 16 out of 120 Knesset members were women.

34

WOMEN OF THE MIDDLE EAST

Golda Meir, Israel's former Prime Minister

It is not impossible for women to get high-ranking government positions. Israeli women have been government ministers. Golda Meir was Israel's prime minister from 1969 to 1974. Women have been mayors and judges on Israel's supreme court for years. Half of the nation's lower court and district court judges are women.

Israel's political parties have supported women in politics. In 2001, the Labor party required that at least 30 percent of its leadership positions be filled by women. The Likud party required that 20 percent of its leaders be women.

In the workforce, 75 percent of women do jobs that are considered "women's work." They are teachers, health care workers, or social workers.

In business, men tend to hold more powerful positions than women. More men are company executives. Male executives also receive better benefits. Men are more likely to get a company car or additional job training than women. In the general workforce, women are paid only about 80 percent of what men are paid per hour. Arab women are paid about 30 percent less than Jewish women.

Women have participated in Israel's military since Biblical times. Currently, both men and women are required to participate in the Israel Defense Forces, or IDF. Once they reach 18, healthy women who do not have children are required to serve one year and nine months in the IDF.

Since 2000, Israeli women have been allowed in every military profession. They train in computer programming and other technical positions. They are now allowed to participate in military combat units as well. In 2001, the first female fighter pilot graduated from Israeli flight school.

Religious guidelines continue to keep many Israeli women in the home. Others take advantage of the rights granted to them by their government. Israel continues to increase opportunities for women in public life. Religious and social customs, however, are often in conflict.

SAUDI ARABIA

S audi Arabia is another Middle Eastern country in which the role of women is based largely on Islamic beliefs. The Saudi Arabian government is a religious monarchy. Its laws are based on the laws of Islam.

Saudi Arabian women have considerably more freedoms than women in some other Islamic countries. Saudi Arabian women have rights to education and employment, and they have choices in marriage. On the other hand, women in Saudi Arabia have fewer civil rights than men.

In Saudi Arabia, girls live at home until they are married. When a girl marries, she moves into her husband's home. A Saudi Arabian woman does not change her name after marriage.

In Saudi Arabia, many marriages are arranged. In some cases, the parents of the prospective bride and groom will arrange a meeting between the man, his father, and the prospective bride's father. Neither the man nor the woman will have seen each other before this time. The intended bride will make a

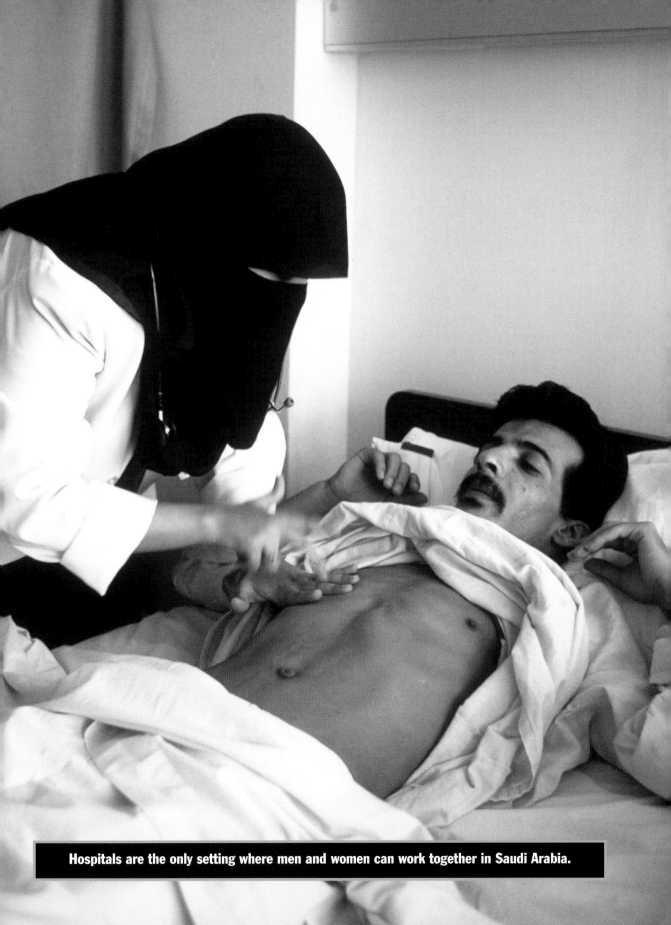

Hospitals are the only setting where men and women can work together in Saudi Arabia.

brief appearance, perhaps to offer the men something to drink. If both the prospective bride and groom agree to the marriage after this brief meeting, a wedding date is set.

Most Saudi Arabian women are free to voice their opinions about their intended husbands. Before a marriage, the woman may write down specific terms. The terms may regard property rights, child custody, or divorce.

Divorce is fairly common in Saudi Arabia. In 2001, Saudi Arabian courts granted an average of 25 to 35 divorces a day.

Saudi Arabian women and girls make up half of the students in Saudi Arabia's schools and universities. Girls and boys go to separate schools. In Saudi Arabian society, men and women are always kept apart from each other in public.

Women in Saudi Arabia are allowed to work outside the home, but women make up less than six percent of the total workforce. They are not allowed to work in fields related to engineering, law, or journalism. Most job opportunities for women are in health care or education. A few women hold high positions in companies.

Laws forbid men and women from interacting with one another unless they are related. This makes working difficult for

Saudi Arabian women. The only place that unrelated men and women are allowed to work side by side is in the hospitals.

Saudi Arabian women are separated from men everywhere they go. Restaurants have special sections for women and families. Banks have special branches just for women. Even at Saudi Arabian weddings, the bride and females will celebrate in a separate room from the husband and men.

Women have little influence in the Saudi Arabian government. In 1999, women were finally allowed to attend meetings of the National Assembly, which advises the monarchy. Women were allowed to view the meeting from a balcony, but they were not allowed to join any discussion. The highest political position that a woman has held in Saudi Arabia was Assistant Secretary in the Ministry of Education. She was a member of the royal family.

Neither women nor men have voting rights in Saudi Arabia. Its government is led by a king. Only members of the royal family can be leaders.

Women in Saudi Arabia are required to wear long cloaks that cover them from head to toe, except for their faces. These cloaks are called abayas. Women who do not follow the dress code can be lashed.

Women in Saudi Arabia have been banned from driving since 1990. Specific taxis have been declared women's taxis. Women are not allowed to travel without permission from a husband or father.

In Saudi Arabia, women are required to follow strict religious laws. Saudi Arabian people believe, as do many Muslims, that the most important place for a woman is in her home.

Women in the Middle East are subject to many religious and social laws. The degree to which women are restricted depends on the country in which they live. Restrictions on women range from dress codes to laws regulating transportation. Many Middle Eastern countries are taking steps to broaden women's rights while maintaining religious laws.

TIMELINE

1956	Egyptian women get the right to vote. A bill also allows them to nominate themselves to the National Assembly.
1963	Iranian women are given the right to vote and to run for office for the first time.
1969-1974	Golda Meir serves as Israel's first and only female Prime Minister.
1979	Iranian Revolution brings the Ayatollah Khomeini into power. He enforces the strict dress code, hijab, on women. He leads Iran under a theocratic government.
1990	Saudi Arabian women are prohibited from driving cars.
1997	In Iran, Shahla Habibi is elected the President's Advisor on Women's Affairs. This is the highest government post ever held by an Iranian woman.
1996-2001	Taliban enforces an Islamic fundamentalist government in Afghanistan. Women are not allowed outside their homes without a burqa and a male family member as an escort.
1999	Women are allowed to observe the Saudi Arabian National Assembly from a balcony. They may present questions to a council member before the meeting, but may not participate in the discussion.
2000	Egypt passes a law allowing women the right to divorce their husbands. They also get the right to file for child support.
2001	Israel's first female fighter pilot graduates from the Israel Air Force pilot course. Afghan women and girls are allowed back into schools after the Taliban government is forced out by U.S. forces.
2003	On January 9, an Iranian soccer club began allowing women to watch soccer games in its Tehran stadium. Women had previously been banned from any sports events.

FAST FACTS

- Egyptian women stay in the house for 40 days after they give birth to a new baby. A woman's female relatives take care of the baby and the new mother during this time.

- In the 1970s and 1980s, women in Afghanistan wore clothes much like people in the United States were wearing.

- Egyptian girls know how to cook most of the family's major dishes by the time they are 15 years old.

- Under Taliban rule, Afghan women could be beaten or shot for being outside of their homes without a male family member.

- In many Muslim countries, women are required to wear veils on their heads. Some have stricter dress codes that require women to wear veils or capes that cover them from head to toe.

- In Saudi Arabia, men and women are segregated in public. They eat in different rooms in restaurants. Women and men celebrate in separate rooms at weddings.

- In Saudi Arabia, grocery stores close during prayer times. The lights are dimmed and doors locked. No one may check out until the prayer time is done.

- In Iran, it is legal for girls to marry once they reach nine years old.

- Islam allows a man to have up to four wives if he can financially support them and treat them well. This practice is common in some Middle Eastern countries, but varies from place to place.

- Women were first allowed into the Israel Air Force in 1997. Since then, four women have completed the pilot course. One of them graduated as a fighter pilot.

WEB SITES
WWW.ABDOPUB.COM

Would you like to learn more about Women of the Middle East? Please visit www.abdopub.com to find up-to-date Web site links about Women of the Middle East and the World in Conflict. These links are routinely monitored and updated to provide the most current information available.

Many Middle Eastern women wear veils in public.

GLOSSARY

Afghanistan:

A country in the Middle East.

agriculture:

Farming.

appropriate:

Acceptable.

burqa:

A garment that some Islamic women are required to wear in public. This covers them from head to toe.

drastic:

Extreme.

harass:

Torment.

impaired:

Lessened or weakened.

Kabul:

The capital city of Afghanistan.

Middle East:

A region of the world that includes part of southwest Asia and northeast Africa.

mosque:

The building where Muslims worship.

Muslim:

Someone who practices Islam.

parliament:

A group of people organized to make laws for a country.

scholarship:

Financial aid given to a student so that he or she may go to school.

segregate:

Separate.

Shari'a law:

Islamic law.

Sunni:

The original Sunni Muslims believed that they should vote for Mohammad's successor. They choose their religious leaders.

Taliban:

The Islamic fundamentalist group that ruled parts of Afghanistan according to strict Koran interpretation.

Western:

Nations in the western hemisphere that are largely Christian dominated.

INDEX